THE Fundraiser's MEASURING STICK

America's Topselling Fundraising Books

Fund Raising Realities
Every Board Member Must Face

A 1-Hour Crash Course on Raising Major Gifts for Nonprofit Organizations

David Lansdowne

From the first page, you and your board will be hooked on this one-hour-to-read gem.

The warmth, encouragement, the perfectly tuned examples, and easy readability make for an inviting package that draws you in at once.

Without wasting a word, Lansdowne distills the essence of big-gifts fundraising into 43 "realities," and explains each principle and technique in a way board members will understand immediately.

Put this classic in your board's hands, in their orientation packet, in their annual meeting folder, in their workshop handouts. Put it anywhere you need the art of fundraising illuminated in a masterful, uncomplicated, and engaging way.

ASKING

A 59-Minute Guide to Everything Board Members, Volunteers, and Staff Must Know to Secure the Gift

Jerold Panas

It ranks right up there with public speaking. Nearly all of us fear it. And yet it's critical to the success of our organizations. Asking for money. It makes even the stout-hearted quiver.

But now comes a book, *Asking,* and short of a medical elixir, it's the next best thing for emboldening board members, volunteers, and staff to ask with skill, finesse … and powerful results.

The No. 1 bestselling fundraising book of all time, *Asking* convincingly shows that it doesn't take stellar sales skills to be an effective asker. Nearly everyone can be successful if they follow Panas' step-by-step guidelines.

Emerson & Church, Publishers
www.emersonandchurch.com

THE Fundraiser's MEASURING STICK

Sizing Up the Attributes Board Members, Volunteers, and Staff Must Cultivate to Secure Major Gifts

JEROLD PANAS

First printed in February 2016

Printed in the United States of America

This text is printed on acid-free paper.

Emerson & Church, Publishers
15 Brook Street – Medfield, MA 02052
Tel. 508-359-0019

www.emersonandchurch.com

Library of Congress Cataloging-in-Publication Data

Names: Panas, Jerold, author.

Title: The fundraiser's measuring stick : sizing up the attributes board members, volunteers, and staff must cultivate to secure big gifts / Jerold Panas.

Description: Medfield, Massachusetts : Emerson & Church, Publishers, 2016.

Identifiers: LCCN 2015045794 | ISBN 9781889102566 (pbk. : alk. paper)

Subjects: LCSH: Fund raising.

Classification: LCC HG177 .P36 2016 | DDC 658.15/224—dc23 LC record available at http://lccn.loc.gov/2015045794

Contents

To the hundreds of thousands of board members and staff who give their heart and soul to their organization. You dream the unthinkable. Attempt the impossible. You provide the scholarships. Feed the hungry. Build the buildings. Furnish the equipment. Find the cures. To use Ernest Hemingway's salute, you will forever be "The winner and undisputed champion."

Chapter 1

The Great Ones

I've never really kept track.

In my years of consulting, I suppose I've worked with thirty thousand fundraisers, both volunteer and professional. Perhaps as many as fifty thousand.

They come in all sizes and shapes and ethnic backgrounds. Tall, short. Heavy, thin. I've seen it all.

I want to describe for you two I've worked with who are utterly different in style and approach. Each was powerfully effective.

When Golda Meir was prime minister of Israel, she sent a young fundraiser to the United States to raise money for Israel and Jewish causes. His name was Aryeh Nesher.

For two decades, Nesher raised funds and trained hundreds of leaders of Jewish Federations in the art of raising money. His art. His method. In Jewish circles, the name Aryeh Nesher is legendary.

Nesher's type of fundraising was rough and tumble, in your face, laced with unforgiving guilt. When someone said, "I'll need time to think it over," his response would strip bark from a tree. I came to know him when he was a volunteer no longer on Israel's payroll.

I was once with a wealthy Jewish leader who said, "Nesher was the only guy I ever threw out of my office. But first, he got the gift."

Now let me describe a total opposite.

Dr. Vartan Gregorian is now president of the Carnegie Corporation. When I first met him, he was president of the New York Public Library. When Vartan assumed the helm of the library, it was moribund. To save money, the storied institution was closed two days a week and in the evenings.

"What Vart did," the chairman of the library board told me, "was comparable to turning the *Queen Mary* around in a bathtub."

One day I'm sitting with Vartan in his office. We're talking about the extraordinary success he's had in securing funds. He raised hundreds of millions of dollars in a very short time.

I tell him he saved the library and that everyone talks about his amazing prowess in raising money. "The truth is," Vartan says, "I never ask for money. I can't remember that I've ever asked for a gift."

I'm incredulous.

"I simply talk with people," he continues. "I tell them what we have is an extraordinary cathedral of scholarship and culture. It's unequaled anywhere in the world. Filled with treasures and one-of-a-kinds.

"I create the dream and the inspiration. When I finish, I never have to ask. They offer me money. 'How much would you like?' they ask."

Here's proof that Vartan isn't kidding.

We go from his office to lunch at his favorite Armenian restaurant. We're sitting by a window looking out on Third Avenue.

A woman walking down the street peers in and spots him. She comes rushing inside.

"Dr. Gregorian, I haven't seen you for ages," she says, excusing herself for interrupting. "Please come see me. I want to give you some money." They hug. She leaves.

"See what I mean?" he says to me.

The great fundraisers I've met all share certain qualities. That includes Nesher and Gregorian, who are poles apart in their styles and approaches.

In the following pages, I'm going to share with you the roster of attributes, talents, and skills that allow the great fundraisers, volunteer or staff, to stand head and shoulders over all the others.

Chapter 2

A Love Affair

The great fundraisers, I've come to learn, experience unbridled joy in what they're doing. It's a love affair. "Etched in the heart," as Camus said. They're passionate about their service and their organizations. And it shows. There's an irrational exuberance—joy inexpressible.

In one of his speeches, Will Rogers said, "If you want to be successful, it's pretty simple. There are only four things to keep in mind:

"i) Know what you're doing, ii) Love what you're doing, iii) Believe in what you're doing, iv) And be passionate about it. Head over heels."

Some think of fundraising as "the profession of pain." Those few board members, volunteers, and staff won't succeed. They're carrying baggage far too heavy. The great fundraisers have the fervor and spirit of a missionary.

Let me tell you about Malin Burnham. He's among San Diego's most highly recognized, most highly esteemed leaders. Stand on any street corner in this southern California city, look in any direction, and you'll see Malin's handiwork. His list of achievements stretches from here to forever. Among the honors: the San Diego Business Hall of Fame, Philanthropist of the Year, Civic Entrepreneur of the Year, Mr. San Diego, and the Gold Spike Award from Stanford University. Oh, and did I mention that Malin has chaired nine major nonprofits and has co-founded 14 organizations in his career, most providing direct benefit to San Diego.

"After all these years, it's my love for the city and its people that keeps me going," he tells me.

Individuals like Malin are evidence that success in raising money is due less to mechanics than enthusiasm for the mission. Less to intelligence than zeal. In fact, if inviting others to share the vision isn't fun for you, you might begin looking for another cause or line of work.

Chapter 3

Resolve Melts Constraints

I love the story about Roger Bannister. It was more than sixty years ago that he broke the four-minute mile. In 1954 that was an unthinkable feat.

But Bannister felt otherwise. "I knew the morning of the race I would do it," he said. "I was resolute. I knew it was possible."

Here's what makes his record shattering all the more astounding. In the next twelve months, four other runners also eclipsed the presumably impossible feat. Since then, hundreds have.

The explanation is that four minutes represented a mental barrier, not a physical constraint. When Bannister broke through the intellectual wall, the world's runners realized such a time wasn't beyond their reach. All that was required was resolve.

The lesson is quite clear. Negative thinking limits performance.

Those of us in philanthropy understand that success is also a long race, one conducted in inches. It is many short races, one after another. We face rejection and refusal head-on and respond with even greater dedication and determination. There are always obstacles in our work. Life is like that. Always supplying thorns with the roses.

"My greatest attribute is persistence," said the 76-year-old Japanese artist Hokusai. "I never stop. I never give up. All that I made before the age of 65 is not worth counting. At 73, I began to understand the true meaning of animals, plants, trees, birds, fish, and insects. At 90, I will enter into the true secret of things. At 110, everything, every dot, will live."

You could say persistence is biting off more than you can chew—and then giving it a good noshing.

Chapter 4

NOW!

Carpe Diem is an ancient Latin phrase that means "Seize the day" (a more literal translation is "Pluck the day"). That's our credo in philanthropy. Lay siege to the moment.

If anyone embodies that sentiment, it's Jim Haslam, founder of Pilot, the convenience centers and travel stops throughout the nation. It's one of the largest privately owned companies in the United States.

When I first met Jim, I asked him who he thought should chair the capital campaign for the University of Tennessee. "I should," he said.

I was shocked. I don't often have someone instantly volunteer to lead a major campaign.

Jim did indeed chair the Campaign for Tennessee. And gave generously. Over the years, he's given tens of millions to the UT–Knoxville as well as other important causes.

Jim wasn't an easy man to work with. He wanted things done immediately. He practiced TNT—Today, Not Tomorrow. But he was a great chair. He knew how to seize the day, and the $1 billion campaign went over goal.

Like Jim, to be an effective fundraiser you can't put things off. The well-being of your organization depends on you.

> They were going to be all they promised to be.
> Tomorrow.
> None would work more effectively, you'd see.
> Tomorrow.
>
> A donor of many years, one they knew,
> Would be glad of a contact—and needed it, too.
> On her they would call, to see what they could do.
> Tomorrow.
>
> Each morning they stacked the letters
> they'd write.
> And resolved to work with all their might.
> Tomorrow.
>
> The greatest of fundraisers they might have been,
> The world would have opened its heart to them.
> But they moved on and faded from view.

And all they left when their task was through,
Was a mountain of work they intended to do.
Tomorrow.

Chapter 5

Selling the Dream

Peter Drucker was arguably the nation's greatest thinker and writer on management. What he said about success is immediately transferable to philanthropy.

I'm paraphrasing, but Drucker emphasized that the responsibility of a skilled fundraiser, whether staff or volunteer, is thinking through the organization's mission, defining and establishing it clearly and visibly. And then communicating the vision and the dreams.

Elie Wiesel writes, "God made human beings because God loves stories. And our lives are the stories He tells."

In your role as fundraiser, you're a storyteller, too. The Bible says to "never lack in dreams, but be aglow and on fire."

Donors want to know why they should give. And especially why should they give *now*. And why have you chosen them to make a gift? You, the dream weaver, must answer these questions.

Edwin Meese was attorney general under Ronald Reagan. He's now co-chair of the Reagan Ranch, a division of Young America's Foundation.

While president, Ronald Reagan and Nancy visited Rancho del Cielo every opportunity they could (some envious Democrats said, "Too often!"). At the time Reagan said, "I'm not certain the Ranch is heaven, but I do know it has the same zip code."

To really understand our fortieth president, Meese says, you have to visit the ranch. "You see President Reagan everywhere you look—in the living room, the bedroom, the saddle room, the pond. Everywhere.

"Come with me," says Meese. "This is where the president carved his initials and Nancy's in a tree.

"Take a look at the pond," he continues, "It's quite a story." Meese is selling the dream. It's irresistible. Pretty soon, you have the feeling he has his hand in your pocket!

The pond is small, no more than forty feet in diameter. It's at the side of the house.

Prior to one of his visits, the president had a huge hole dug and filled it with water. Presto! A pond. Then Reagan bought a row boat that he hid from Nancy.

"In the morning," Meese says, "the president places the boat in the pond and invites Nancy to get in. To the middle of the pond he rows.

"He puts down the oars. Takes her hands in his. Affirms his love for her and proposes again."

With stories like these, Meese is the greatest fund-raiser for the ranch. And just like him, it's your role to inspire the hopes of everyone you call on. John Paul II said these words: *Nolite Timere. Somniare Aude*—Be not afraid. Dare to dream.

Oh yes, and there's a certain way to tell when you've woven the dream for your donor, when a gift is imminent. It's when he or she turns to you and says, "I believe."

Chapter 6

The Itch to Win

Beth Pfeiffer is trustee emeritus of Wellesley College, regarded as one of the most prestigious among women's colleges and one of the most outstanding liberal arts institutions in the nation.

Beth chaired the college's highly successful capital campaign in the 1990s. "When I take something on," she tells me, "I take it on to win. It was the same when the president asked me for my gift. If you want to be successful, you have to lead the way."

Beth made the largest personal gift in her life (she prefers I not mention the amount). "How could I ask others to give if I didn't light the way?" She not only gave, she made calls—scores of them.

Like Beth, great fundraisers set forth on a journey resolved to succeed. The powers they need are in place. The *arête,* the excellence sought by the ancient Greeks, is vibrating with potential.

Another individual like Beth is Michael Ainslie. I knew him first as chair of the campaign for the Royal Poinciana Chapel in Palm Beach, Florida.

In the 1880s, the railroad baron Henry Flagler built a magnificent hotel—the Royal Poinciana—that could accommodate five hundred guests. Wanting a place of worship for his guests, he included a chapel.

As with any structure, repairs inevitably come due. The chapel chose Michael to head the restoration effort, and the goal of $6.5 million was surpassed. He then headed the campaign for the Palm Beach Day Academy with the same resolve and success.

"What is it," I ask Michael, "that makes you such a successful campaign chair?"

"There's something that's been true since I can remember," says Michael. "I long to win. There's no queue for second place. I take on campaigns the same way. I dedicate myself, call on others for gifts, and recruit leaders to work with me."

There's a metaphor I believe applies to the will to win. It's the mountain climber who's continually tossing a grappling hook ahead of him. He perseveres. Then he pulls himself up. Finally he reaches the top, the mountain peak.

Vince Lombardi never uttered the famous quote attributed to him (it was spoken by Henry Russell "Red" Sanders, coach of the 1954 UCLA football team that won the national championship). What Lombardi actually said was, "Winning isn't everything. But wanting to win is." It's not as dramatic, but it's a lot closer to the right idea for board and staff fundraisers.

There's always the high level of optimism, of chasing a whale with a harpoon and a jar of tartar sauce.

Chapter 7

The Magic of Courage

Icarus flew so close to the sun that the wax on his wings melted, plunging him back to Earth. From the pinnacle of achievement to the banality of failure.

The decline was heartbreaking. Yet he experienced a high known to few. Perhaps the tragic thing would have been if he hadn't dared the flight in the first place.

The great fundraisers understand that when they face resistance, when a hurdle appears, they can and eventually will soar over it.

Let me tell you about Mary Kay Ash, a woman with more courage than anyone I've ever worked with. You may know her best for her company, Mary Kay Cosmetics. She's one of America's business giants and among a handful of the greatest women entrepreneurs.

"From early childhood, I was infused with a can-do attitude," she told me. "I felt there was no mountain I couldn't climb."

With little capital she opened a storefront in Dallas, calling her new company Mary Kay Cosmetics International. She was the only employee. In time it grew to 3.5 million beauty consultants.

I witnessed Mary Kay's courage when I worked with the Wadley Research Institute in Dallas. She was on the board and later worked on the campaign. At the time she was fighting cancer, but it didn't deter her a bit from making calls on donors. I asked about her fortitude.

"There are some people who die with their music unplayed," she told me. "That won't be me."

In Theodore Roosevelt's *The Man in the Arena* speech, there's a glowing statement about courage that speaks to Mary Kay's mettle. "The credit belongs to the man who is actually in the arena," Roosevelt says, "whose face is marred by dust and sweat and blood; who strives valiantly, who errs and comes up short again and again—because there is not effort without error and shortcoming."

Not many find it easy to ask for a gift. But it's the ability to make the call and ask—in the presence of trepidation and butterflies—that marks the successful fundraiser.

Heed the words of General George S. Patton: "You will never know the thrill of life, until you hear the whistle of the bullets."

Chapter 8

Outsized Optimism

Recently, I had an opportunity to meet with Larry Ellison on behalf of a client. Ellison is the co-founder and genius behind Oracle. He told me it wasn't always easy for his software company. At times, it still isn't.

During its darkest days, some closest to Ellison doubted Oracle would rebound and survive. But his resolve never wavered.

When I asked what made the difference, he said acting confident even when he wasn't. "You have to be an optimist," he said. "Eliminate the words 'I don't think I can' from your vocabulary. Substitute 'I know I can.'"

Here's the story of another optimist, one who woke up practically every day singing "Oh, What a Beautiful Morning." It was so loud it practically shook the windows is what his wife Helen tells me.

I'm speaking of the late Norvel Young, former president and later chancellor of Pepperdine University in Malibu, California. Norvel was responsible for moving

Pepperdine from downtown Los Angeles to Malibu—one of the nation's most breathtaking campuses.

Under his leadership, Pepperdine grew from a small college with 950 students to a full-fledged university with an enrollment of nearly 7,500.

Norvel was the most highly regarded and most visible of his faith, the Church of Christ, when he headed for a fall. To the deepest of depths.

Due to the unrelenting stress of his job, Norvel became a closet drinker. Worst of all, in a church that doesn't tolerate alcohol.

As he was on his way to a meeting, Norvel's car violently struck another. Two were killed. He willingly admitted consuming a quart of vodka shortly before the accident.

Crushed by guilt, Norvel wondered why he hadn't been killed in the accident. He kept thinking of the two older women and the driver.

He was sentenced to a year in jail—but the judge, not without controversy, suspended the sentence on the condition Norvel take a six-month leave of absence from his duties at Pepperdine and perform public service, which he did.

I came to know Norvel upon his return as chancellor. We were involved in the school's largest campaign ever. And even though Pepperdine had never conducted a major gifts campaign, Norvel's optimism carried the day.

I remember him telling me, "I'm a believer. A born-again optimist. I'm convinced if you build within your team a feeling of confidence, you can accomplish miracles."

And we did.

There are always naysayers. They tell you, "If anything can go wrong, it will. If anything can't go wrong, it still will." You know better. Your life is an exclamation, not an explanation.

For some volunteers and staff, seeking charitable gifts grinds them down. Others it polishes. It all depends on your attitude.

Zerizus is a Hebrew word that means no matter the odds, no matter how difficult—you barrel ahead with a sense of calm, confidence, and total optimism. As they say, like a Methodist with four aces.

"Only you can make yourself what you decide you want to be," Camus said. That's how you win. You make a covenant of what you want to achieve.

Chapter 9

A Flair for Leadership

Forgive me for generalizing, but I'm with Frederick L. Collins when he says, "I find there are two types of people in the world: Those who come into a room and say 'Here I am,' and those who come in and say, 'Ah, there you are.'"

Almost always, the latter attitude characterizes a leader.

I'm sitting with Father Hesburgh, the president of Notre Dame from 1952 to 1987. The walls of his office are lined with dozens of photographs of him with the nation's presidents—from Franklin Roosevelt to Barack Obama. Father is revered.

"I'll explain what I feel leadership is all about," he tells me, "and it's surprisingly simple. I bring a vision of where I want to take the university and I communicate it. That's what it's all about."

Leaders divine and define the future. They articulate their vision in such a way that it inspires others to join them in the adventure.

This quality of leadership is also found in Dr. Frank Cerra. For years, he was the head of health sciences at the University of Minnesota.

In his role as senior vice president, Cerra raised hundreds of millions of dollars for his division, the largest in the university. Now as chair of the Development Committee for St. Vladimir's Seminary in Yonkers, New York, he exerts the same leadership qualities, steering the seminary in the largest campaign in its history.

When Cerra became dean of the medical school in 1996, it was regarded as a fine place. In truth it was mediocre. And rife with scandals. When Cerra left fourteen years later, it was and still is rated among the top ten in the country. A research powerhouse with a $1.2 billion budget.

"I credit Frank with the growth and national prominence," says university president Dr. Robert Bruininks. "It's his leadership. When Frank weighs in on an issue you feel it. And respond."

Let me conclude by saying a word about Dr. Denton Cooley. In 1968, he performed America's first successful human heart transplant. Cooley and his associates have completed nearly 120,000 open-heart operations—more than any other group in the world.

The Texas Heart Institute, where Cooley operates, is housed in St. Luke's Medical Center in Houston, a client of ours at the time.

Working on a feature story, a journalist shadowed the cardiologist for a week. One morning, scrubbed and ready to enter the operating room, Cooley, the ever inspiring leader, stopped to talk for several minutes with the individual mopping the floor. Then he went into surgery.

Immediately, the journalist approached the custodian and asked what he and Cooley had talked about. "We talk that way every morning," said the custodian. "I'm part of the team. You know, around here we all save lives."

Chapter 10

Wondrous Possibilities

At heart, every obstacle is an opportunity waiting to reveal itself. Such is the attitude of great fundraisers. They see a problem through a kaleidoscope. A twist here, a turn there, and the pieces display brilliant, harmonious patterns.

Father Hesburgh, whom I mentioned in the last chapter, told me his secret for solving a sticky problem.

"Usually, if I don't come up with a solution it means I don't really understand the problem," he said. "So I explain it to someone and I listen to their response. Mostly what I'm doing though is listening to myself discuss it. Eventually, the solution comes into focus."

Dr. Gregory Alan Thornbury is the spirited and exuberant president of The King's College in New York. He's a writer and speaker on philosophy, theology, education, spirituality, and public thought. I doubt he understood what pitfalls were in store for him when he assumed the presidency of King's. Let's count them.

A mounting deficit, four years in the running. No data records. Major donors who hadn't been called on for years. Sky-high donor attrition. A faculty . . . well, I should keep that to myself.

But none of this seems to faze Greg. All he sees are the opportunities. "Just think of the possibilities," he says. "I can't believe how lucky I am. We're here in this great city. With a mission unlike any college in the metropolitan area. Very bright students. And unlimited potential. All we can go is up."

Under his leadership, the college has flourished. Neglected donors are called upon for the first time in years. Enrollment is increasing. And there's a revitalized board. Greg never saw the problems. All he could see were the possibilities.

Similarly, one of the greatest fundraisers I've ever worked with, George Denney, chair of the campaign for the Park School in Brookline, Massachusetts, told me if you hit the bull's-eye every time with one of your solutions, you're either coming up with the wrong answer, or the target's too close.

To think "impossible" strangles an idea at birth. Too often, it's timidity of spirit that leads to certain failure.

Of course, you may falter. But as Robert Schuller said, "If there exists no possibility of failure, then victory is meaningless."

Chapter 11

Action Above All

Knowing the best approach to a potential donor isn't a tidy process. The great fundraisers understand this. They acknowledge that research is essential, but they also realize that, as Shakespeare says, action is eloquence.

Perry Pepper is the outstanding CEO of the Chester County Hospital in West Chester, Pennsylvania. We're discussing someone on his staff.

"You know, Jerry, I like Wally [not his real name] a lot. He works hard and is a fearless asker. But it worries me that much of what he does is based on guesswork."

Here's what happened.

We're conducting a campaign for $40 million. It's called *Exceeding Expectations.* We recruited a remarkable cabinet for the campaign. Lots of money. Power. Influence. The wealthiest of the group is Bob (again, not his real name).

I get a call from Wally in the Development Department. He's very excited. "Jerry, I'm going to call on Bob for his gift," he tells me.

"I think it may be too soon," I say. "We just recruited him."

"No. I believe he's ready," Wally insists.

"I think it's a mistake," I tell Wally. "How much are you thinking of asking?"

"$20 million."

"Good grief, why that much? As I recall, he's never been involved in the hospital and he's never given."

"Well, he's got the money. I just read in *Forbes* that his net worth is $4 billion."

"Wally, why don't you call on him but not ask for money. Probe. Build a relationship. Have you done any research?"

"Of course. He and his wife were co-chairs of their daughter's school campaign. They gave two and a half million."

"That's a long way from $20 million," I say.

"I feel it in my gut. I'm going to do it."

Wally made the ask. I couldn't dissuade him. And it was disastrous. Soon after I get a call from Perry, the CEO.

"I just had a call from Bob. He's resigning from the cabinet and wants out of the campaign. He's upset with

Wally. Bob said he planned on giving, but not nearly $20 million. I'm hoping we can calm him down."

As I'm sure you already know, what Wally should have allowed was time for cultivation. And for a gift even approaching that size, Perry should have made the call. A major donor wants to hear the CEO's vision and dreams.

Unlike Wally, the fundraiser with the right instincts can analyze a complex situation. Somehow a solution and a design are developed that cut through the fat and get to the very heart of the situation.

Katherine Graham, the famous publisher of the *Washington Post,* was like that. I was privileged to work with her briefly when we conducted a campaign for the hospital on Martha's Vineyard, where she had a summer home.

"I quickly found out," Katherine told me on one of my visits, "that things don't stand still. I have to make fast decisions. They have to be based on facts you can trust. Then you have to push ahead."

That's what Katherine did as publisher. She presided over the *Post* and played an integral role in unveiling the Watergate conspiracy.

As a philanthropist, Katherine was a close friend of the Museum of Modern Art in New York where she was honored as a recipient of the David Rockefeller Award for enlightened generosity and advocacy of cultural and civic endeavors. She also prided herself on backing Send-A-Kid-To-Camp, an organization which sent inner-city children of the District of Columbia to summer camp.

Just like Graham, great fundraisers size up the situation, make resolute decisions, and move forward with confidence.

Chapter 12

Doing Whatever It Takes

There is a certain majesty to hard work. Even the weariness it leaves is exhilarating. The great fundraisers know this.

Take your cue from Ben Feldman, insurance salesman par excellence (the Feldman Endowment honors and perpetuates the memory of the industry legend). He sold life insurance policies with a face value of some $1.5 billion and transformed his industry.

What made Feldman so successful? Harry Hohn, chairman of New York Life, suggested an answer to those who gathered for the salesman's funeral: "Ben really felt everyone in the world was underinsured."

Feldman would do whatever it took to insure people. After weeks of trying to get in to see a prominent real estate developer in Youngstown, Ohio, "Ben finally asked the secretary to take five $100 bills into her boss—to buy five minutes of his time. 'If I don't have a good idea for him,' Ben told her, 'he can keep the money.' He got in, and sold a $14 million policy."

Endurance like Feldman's is at the core of all who wish to be successful. "There are a lot of factors in making the sale," he said, "but nothing is more important than the time you put in." Feldman worked twelve-hour days, six or seven days a week.

I'm reminded of Kemmons Wilson, founder of Holiday Inn. We were doing a campaign in Memphis for the YMCA. He was no longer active in the business but his shadow was everywhere.

Kemmons regaled me with stories. One I remember particularly. "I never went to college. Never had time," he said. "I went right to work.

"I was invited by my high school to give the graduating class the secret for my success. I told them 'When you get into business, I want you to work only a half a day every day. And I don't care if it's the first 12 hours or the second 12 hours."

I'm not advocating you become a workaholic. On the contrary, balance in one's life is essential. But I have found is that the most successful fundraisers, *when they are working,* are passionate about what they do.

As novelist Rebecca West wrote: "Life ought to be a journey of action and adventures. To avoid passion is death. Apathy is the deadly sin. To be successful in your work, you must abandon yourself to your passion."

Charles Steinmetz, the genius inventor, said he was successful because he succeeded in getting his actual work down to thirty minutes a day—which left him eighteen uninterrupted hours for engineering and just sheer fun.

Chapter 13

Ignited with Energy

Energy is a rare quality but available to all. Each of the great fundraisers I know has it in abundance. There's a reservoir that seems never to ebb.

B. Joseph White is the former president of the University of Illinois, and an extraordinary strategist and fundraiser. He's emphatic when he speaks with me on the subject.

"There are some days when I'm simply dragging. That's the truth of it. But I screw myself up. I make myself energetic."

The great ones like White understand what it means to push against their own capacity until a surge of energy takes them beyond what they thought was possible.

The same with Melanie Sabelhaus. "She makes coffee nervous!" is how I would sum up Melanie. Few volunteers have as much stamina as this remarkable woman.

She and her husband were co-chairs of the United Way campaign in Baltimore. Currently, she's vice chair of the American Red Cross, responsible for nationwide fundraising strategies. Add to that board memberships at Ohio University, Johns Hopkins University, and the College of Notre Dame in Maryland.

She managed to fit this all in even while serving as the deputy administrator of the U.S. Small Business Administration. Incidentally, she also founded her own real estate firm involving interim properties, which later went public.

How does she do it? Melanie tells me it's partly in her genes. "But there are some days I need to push myself because I know how important it is to demonstrate energy. It's contagious. When I call on people for their gifts, I know it helps."

I conducted a study of major donors to learn what they wanted most in the volunteer or staff calling on them. Guess what led the list? You guessed it. Energy.

Angle of repose, which is the name of Wallace Stegner's Pulitzer Prize–winning novel, is a technical phrase used by mining engineers. It describes the angle at which sliding dirt and debris come to rest. A full stop.

The essayist and short story writer Joseph Epstein says the phrase is "too good to be wasted on dirt." It should be used for humans. He says for many it's descriptive of their attitude and existence. "People with energy," writes Epstein, "rule the world."

It takes someone with incredible drive to throw himself totally and completely into the development of a great cause that counts. Like Robert Schuler, who built the Crystal Cathedral. He was the most recognized television evangelist of his time.

"Even when I'm tired," he told me when I met with him in his office, "something inside keeps driving me on. I have a tremendous amount of energy."

And if you didn't? I asked.

"We'd have an empty collection plate," he said.

Chapter 14

Unfailing Memory

Most of the great fundraisers I know are well-organized with tight schedules. But another attribute that stands out is their prodigious memories. Without exception, almost all of them exhibit this.

"I have 1,200 professional librarians on my staff, and I know them all." That's Vartan Gregorian speaking. I introduced you to him earlier.

"You know each one?" I ask.

"Yes," he tells me, "and I know their spouses and children and where they live and where they went to school."

Vartan exhibited the same remarkable memory when he was president of Brown University. Even down to the names and backgrounds of the men and women on the Alumni Council and Student Council.

"I wouldn't think of calling on a donor," he says, "if I didn't know everything about them. It would be rude of me. And not very effective."

Another highly regarded individual in the field—winner of many awards and citations—is William Sturtevant. He headed the philanthropy office at the University of Illinois. In the past few years he's been special counsel to the president.

At any given time, Bill had nearly two hundred major donors in his portfolio. Too many for most, but he somehow handled the load. What's remarkable is Bill's recall. He remembered everything about his supporters, down to the smallest details. Wedding anniversaries, hobbies, favorite meals, and even the name of the cat.

It's no surprise that during his three decades of service Bill was monumentally successful. He was directly involved in securing over $600 million in major gifts. And, during the University of Illinois's recently completed campaign, Bill, with his unrivalled sense of recall, guided the effort to secure 65 gifts of $5.0 million or more. I'm guessing he even knew the grandchildren's names of each and every one of those donors.

Chapter 15

Steadfast Commitment

"Until one is committed," Goethe wrote, "there is hesitancy, the chance to drop back. The moment one definitely commits oneself, then Providence moves, too."

The great fundraisers I know have unshakable commitment to their organizations. There is a near-militant belief in their missions. Best-selling author Ken Blanchard tells me there's a difference between *interest* and *commitment.*

"When you're interested in your work, you do only what is necessary. When you're committed, it's different. You accept no excuses. Only exceptional results."

The Salvation Army was founded by an extraordinary person, a zealot. "Why should the devil have all of the good songs?" William Booth asked. It was his unmitigated devotion to the cause and unbounded belief in the Army's mission that made the growth of this organization possible.

Fifteen years ago, Dr. James B. Fahner helped found the Hospice of Michigan and its pediatric program which cares for terminally ill children and their families. Currently he serves as division chief of Pediatric Hematology/Oncology at Helen DeVos Children's Hospital in Grand Rapids, Michigan.

For all the years following the creation of the hospice, Jim worked relentlessly for the organization. He has been a member of the board and twice served as chair.

But perhaps his greatest contribution has been his incessant soliciting of funds. "Without question, if it weren't for Dr. Fahner, there would be no Hospice," says Dottie Deremo, retired CEO of the organization.

"I'm shameless about my fundraising," Jim says. "We have an important program and I'm simply asking people to join me in a great cause. We're touching the lives of hundreds—no, thousands—of parents. What could anyone do that would be more important?"

In September 2011, five local families donated $1 million and the program was renamed in honor of its founder. Today the organization is called the Hospice of Michigan James B. Fahner, M.D., Pediatric Hospice Care Program.

Chapter 16

High Touch, Low Tech

Great fundraisers have an appreciation for electronic equipment and software. But they keenly understand the computer doesn't take the place of calling on someone for a gift—not any more than a pencil substitutes for literacy.

Technocrats know "how." But that's not the heart and soul of our work. We know the effectiveness and power of the personal touch.

The high-touch fundraiser transforms a probable donor who talks of *your* organization to one who comes to see it as *our* group.

The esteemed dean of fundraising, Si Seymour, wrote about the importance of personal contact. "I cannot emphasize too strongly how much more effective it is to sit knee to knee when asking for a gift. A phone call doesn't do it. A letter is even worse.

"You don't get milk from a cow by sending a letter. And you don't get milk from calling on the phone. You get milk by sitting next to the cow and milking it."

I hear it all the time—the importance of social media. If Descartes were alive today, he would probably say, as some wag did recently, "I think, therefore I tweet!"

Social media is indeed an essential component of philanthropy. It's the fastest-growing segment in our work. But it still represents only a fraction of the money that's raised (some say 6 percent).

Much of the other 94 percent comes from sitting across from a donor, making your case, and asking him or her to join you in a great cause.

Chapter 17

First Taste of Victory

I've met few who relish the idea of asking for a gift. Not many queue up to solicit. It takes practice and discipline. I find, however, that once they secure their first gift and taste victory, you can't hold solicitors back. They practically lust for the call.

Let me give you an example.

When we recruited Martha Firestone Ford to serve on the board of Ford Hospital in Detroit, she made her position clear. "I'd be proud to serve on the board. And I'll make a large gift. But I won't make calls. Especially, I won't call on any of my friends. Am I perfectly clear?"

"Of course, Martha," I said. I could have pointed out that all board members are expected to solicit, but with someone like Martha you tend to make an exception.

Then something happened to change all that.

There was a key prospect no one on the board knew. No one but Martha. She and Fred are close friends.

When we ask Martha to contact Fred, she threatens to resign from the board. We convince her she won't have to ask for a gift. We just want her make the appointment. With great reluctance, she agrees.

There we are. Colette Murray, vice president at the time, Martha, Fred, and yours truly.

Colette and I are sitting at Fred's desk. Martha is sitting against the wall fifteen feet away. Hands crossed. Lips tight. A scowl on her face.

Colette is describing the need. The urgency. She is selling the dream, speaking of all the lives at stake. I notice that Martha's chair is slowly moving to Fred's desk. Just at the point when Colette is about to ask for the gift, Martha interrupts her.

"Fred, as a personal favor, I'd like you to give $2 million," she says. Martha actually asked. She got caught in the dream.

"Of course, Martha, I will," says Fred, just like that (I wish we had asked for more!). After that meeting, Martha couldn't resist. She wanted to call on everyone.

In much the same way, Harlan Swift, Sr., came to understand what it's like to be a joyous asker. He was president of the Erie County Bank and the chair of one of our campaigns in Buffalo.

"I always felt the importance of giving," Harlan told me. "But I never really understood the joy of asking. Not until I got out there and did it. Before I wasn't eager about it. Now I know my asking is as important as my giving.

"I don't wake up in the morning and think 'What fun, I'll be fundraising today!' But I will tell you I've actually come to enjoy it."

Martha and Harlan are only two examples of hundreds I could give you.

Chapter 18

Soaring Spiritual Values

Not every great fundraiser is a churchgoer, but many demonstrate spiritual values that infuse others with trust and confidence.

Isaiah wrote about this special group: "The Lord shall renew their strength. They will soar like eagles. They will run and not grow weary." I'm convinced the great ones are touched by a higher power.

I'll tell you of one such angel. Her name is Helen Bakalis Nicozisis of Lancaster, Pennsylvania. She and her husband, Louis, have been involved in every major Greek program and campaign, local and national.

Not long ago, Helen was honored for her leadership and philanthropy by Leadership 100. That's a select group of men and women who give $100,000 to a variety of Greek causes in this country.

But it's Helen's involvement in the Orthodox Christian Missionary Center that really stands out. This is a force that provides missionaries for all of the communions of the Orthodox Churches.

Helen was one of the early board members and chaired the board on two occasions, the first lay person and woman to hold the position. She's a fierce, fearless, and indefatigable asker. Her spiritual values and abiding love for the church propel her fundraising activities.

Helen chaired the organization's capital campaign for some five years, leading to the construction of its new headquarters in St. Augustine, Florida.

Just as they do for Helen, spiritual values also figured in the life of John Milton, former vice president of the University of California, Irvine.

His story was not unlike many others I heard.

"I was raised by my grandmother," he tells me one afternoon. "We never went to church. But I can tell you there was a spiritual value permeating our house. We lived by it. You could feel it in everything we did. Growing up, that's who I was.

"At bedtime, Grandma would read us a verse, prayers at meal time, and always a prayer to send us safely to school. She talked to us about values and caring for others. I really think that's why I went into the field."

Saint Paul said that just as a candle cannot burn without fire, man cannot live without a spiritual existence. I find that to be true of the great fundraisers I know.

Chapter 19

Agape

The Greeks had a word for it, now commonly used in English—*agape.* It means unconditional love. Selfless. Of an almost spiritual nature.

I spent a good amount of time with Bart Giamatti when he was president of Yale University. "The truth is," he tells me one day, "I hate being president. Let me rephrase that. If I had to be president anywhere, it would be Yale. That's not the issue. I simply don't like the job. What I want most in life is to be baseball commissioner. That's my goal." (And indeed, he eventually did become baseball commissioner.)

"I don't understand," I say. "You've been president for nearly five years. And you dislike the job?"

He nodded. "Fundraising isn't my favorite sport. I'd prefer to be in the classroom. I stay because I like people. I know through my work here I'm touching many lives. In turn, they touch the lives of thousands. What else could I be doing that would be more important? For me, it's all about people."

Even though Giamatti's dream was to be the head of Major League Baseball, he nevertheless became an extraordinary fundraiser for Yale—raising hundreds of millions. I ask about his particular skill.

"I became good at raising money because of my fondness for those around me. I understood that the money was all about helping our students. And I love my students."

Linus Pauling shared Giamatti's affection for people. I was fortunate to meet the renowned biochemist at lunch one afternoon as we prepared to call on department store magnate, Cyril Magnin, for a gift to the Pauling Institute.

I sat down and to the left of my knife, lined up vertically, were eleven pills and vitamins. I counted them. A few were as large as a quarter.

"Go ahead, take them," commanded Pauling in his booming voice. "They're all for you. Before lunch."

You probably remember Pauling as the raging proponent of Vitamin C for everything from conquering cancer to curing the common cold. He was also a noted peace activist and defender of civil liberties—one of only four individuals to win the Nobel Prize twice.

Like Giamatti, Pauling loved the people around him and showed it on every occasion. I'm convinced that volunteers and staff who don't have this same feeling, this love affair with those in their midst, may actually be at the wrong organization.

Chapter 20

Breaking the Rules

There are times board members and staff must cast aside the strictures. For truly successful fundraisers, conventions and status quo are often hindrances. The people who are crazy enough to think they can change the world are often the ones who do.

The other day I read a fascinating article on barnacles (odd subject, I admit). The piece had a revealing paragraph. The barnacle, I learned, is confronted early on with a decision about where it's going to live the rest of its life. Once it decides, it spends its entire existence with its head cemented to a rock.

For many, it does come to that. But not highly productive fundraisers. They take a hammer to a glass wall of tired ideas while others spend their time polishing the panes.

Most of the great ones think in the future tense. They understand if you're still doing today what you did yesterday, the parade has likely passed you by.

They also understand that a major motivation for those who give is the desire to create change. The donor wants to see things happen, to feel that through his or her gift there will be meaningful results.

Michael Hyatt considers himself an uber change agent. An innovator, an enemy of the status quo. For seven years he was president and CEO of Thomas Nelson Publishing, one of the largest distributors in the nation of Christian books and Bibles.

Recently Hyatt made a substantial gift to one of my clients. I'm at his home in Tennessee talking about the gift.

"Your gift is noteworthy for two reasons," I say. "The first is its extraordinary size. But what's also unusual is you didn't designate how you want your gift to be used. You only said you wanted it to create thoughtful, positive change."

Hyatt, the author of seven books, including the New York Times best seller, *Platform: Get Noticed in a Noisy World,* looks me in the eye. "That's true. I don't want my funds used to perpetuate the same-old same-old," he says with conviction. "I want the organization to try something new. If it fails, so be it. It'll still be worth the effort."

Similarly, in an article in the *Economist,* Bill Gates talked about why he was so successful. "I run like hell," he said, "and then change direction."

He went on to say, "In today's world, to be successful, you must be a change agent." Then he qualified that. No, "you need to be a *change terrorist.*"

Chapter 21

Give and Feel the Glow

I'm sitting in the living room of Marianne McDonald of Rancho Santa Fe, California. She's telling me of the joy giving brings her.

"I tell people I call on that I hope they'll feel the same exhilaration I do when they make a gift," says Marianne. "It lifts my spirits."

She mentions a gift she made to honor her father. "The day I decided to make that gift I couldn't eat, couldn't talk to anyone I was so excited.

"When I went to bed I couldn't sleep a wink. I kept thinking, Dad, you're going to be so proud. In the morning, I got out of bed and saw myself in the mirror. I practically shouted, 'Marianne, you're one hell of a lady.'"

Marianne isn't alone. Almost all donors feel the same joy. You will, too, for as a fundraiser you know the importance of making your own gift.

Let me tell you about Edwin Whitehead. From childhood, he was known as Jack. "I never gave any money away," he tells me. "Not a penny.

"One day I went to my attorney to do some estate planning. During the course of our conversation he asked if I knew how much I was worth. I told him I had no idea. I said we were comfortable."

Several years later Jack sells his company Technicon to Revlon for $400 million (indeed he was comfortable!).

"My attorney says to me, 'Jack, I've been your personal and corporate lawyer for years. You're now one of the wealthiest people in the country. You've never given away a penny in your life. Now that you have all this money it's time to start giving some away. And, actually, there could be a tax advantage.'

"So, yes, I decided I'd start giving. But I'm a businessman, you know, and you don't just start giving money away—you have to think about it and make a plan.

"I took a sheet of paper and drew a line down the middle. On one side, I penciled in the six organizations I was interested in and where I might make a gift. On the other column I listed the reasons I thought I should give to them.

"After about a week of drawing lines and thinking, one organization stood out the most. That's it, I said, that's where I'm going to make my gift.

"I went to my desk, picked up a pen, and wrote a check. For $100. It felt good. So I went to the second organization on my list and I also sent a check for $100.

It was like the top of my head was spinning off. I never knew how good it could feel to give money away."

Well, Jack continued giving and increased the amounts a bit. To Duke University he gave $10 million. To MIT $120 million (you've no doubt heard of the Whitehead Institute). Other oversized gifts followed.

David Baltimore, the Nobel laureate who was the Whitehead Institute's first director, said this: "Jack was an extraordinary man who started with little, built an enormous fortune, and then dedicated himself to using it in an imaginative and personal way that made a major contribution to biomedical research."

Like Jack and Marianne, you'll find it's impossible to give without feeling the glow and the exhilaration of helping to changes the lives of others.

Chapter 22

The Itch for Action

I'm sometimes asked to list the skills of a successful fundraiser. Always on my list is patience. But funny enough I also list impatience. That's because fundraising is more art than science and each situation is different.

Some instances call for prolonged cultivation, taking time to build the relationship. But in some cases there simply isn't time. The call has to be made. That's why I hedge about patience being a virtue.

Bill Wilson is one of the great fundraisers and leaders in Nashville. He comes by it honestly. His father, Pat, led almost every major campaign in the city and for years was chair of Vanderbilt University.

Of the many campaigns Bill spearheaded, the one for the YMCA was perhaps his greatest achievement. The Y at the time enjoyed visibility, but it was second on just about everyone's list.

"The clock was ticking," Bill tells me. "There wasn't time for cultivation. It's not the best way to do it, I know.

But construction was starting on two projects. We had to sell our vision and dreams on the first visit."

Bill and his committee made a list of the top one hundred leaders in Nashville. The emphasis was clearly on those who could make a substantial gift.

"We took them on a bus tour of our centers, gave them lunch, and asked for the gift. That's how quick and simple it was."

Of course Bill doesn't recommend this process for every situation, but it worked in his case.

"What was interesting, by moving as fast as we did, we created a sense of urgency," he says. "Everyone worked faster and harder." The campaign went well over goal.

I concede to no one my strong belief in effective cultivation. But there are instances where the need is urgent. If your house is on fire, you call on your neighbors for a hose.

One such fire was at The King's College, New York City. There were overdue invoices, a bank loan outstanding, and a payroll—all due in two weeks.

It was providential. God sent Allie (Alice) Hanley.

Allie is a fervent member of the college's board. She is passionate, head-over-heels devoted, a whirling dervish. A whole campaign organization wrapped in one person.

In two weeks, Allie called on twenty-two men and women—none had heard from the college in years.

"What could I do?" Allie tells me. "I know I should have made a contact, maybe two or three, before asking for a gift. And it's likely I'd have gotten a larger gift with even a little cultivation. But there simply wasn't time. We were desperate."

Allie raised the necessary funds. The loan was repaid, invoices taken care of, and payroll was met.

Being impatient isn't necessarily a flaw in character. Rather, it can be nothing less than the soul and spirit reaching toward infinity.

Chapter 23

Win-Win-Win

When a donor gives, the organization wins. The donor wins, too, since his or her gift will change lives. And of course there's a third win. The people served by the organization. In essence, the gift keeps giving.

Successful fundraisers understand this. They make certain donors are aware of how important their gifts are. They practice the **BOY** Rule. **B**ecause **O**f **Y**ou.

Few people, no matter how altruistic, are willing to support programs that don't interest them. There has to be an inherent benefit that appeals. Your job as a fundraiser is to a dream merchant—to weave the project into something irresistible. It's not about the cancer center, it's about saving lives. It's not about a camp scholarship, it's about changing a life.

Andrew Carnegie said that if a man dies rich, he has died in disgrace. You help the men and women you call on to understand that it's impossible to take with them what they don't give away.

You also help them understand that their giving causes a ripple effect. A donor's gift affects hundreds, perhaps thousands. And those lives touch others, perhaps hundreds of thousands. The ripples keep growing and expanding.

And, strangely, these donors, as they've told me firsthand, find that what they give comes back to them. In fact, the more they give, the more that comes back.

"I want to give it all away," Denny Sanford told me. He's chairman and CEO of United National Corporation. Sanford made his fortune as the owner of First PREMIER Bank and PREMIER Bankcard, both among the nation's leading credit card providers.

Sanford is making good on his promise. Thus far he's given away more than a billion dollars. "When I die, I want my last check to bounce," he said. "I want it all gone to charity."

But life is like a wheel. "The trouble is," Sanford said, "the more I give away, the more that comes back. It takes all the time I have to give it away."

I once knew a man,
Some thought him mad.
The more he gave away,
The more he had.

Chapter 24

Luck Follows Tenacity

Louis Nizer, author of *My Life in Court,* was one of the nation's most highly esteemed trial attorneys. He was once asked if there was such a thing as luck in trial law. "Yes, but it only comes at three in the morning while I'm doing my research."

All of the successful fundraisers I know speak of the good fortune they have. Luck seems to follow them. Listen to what Father Theodore Hesburgh, president of Notre Dame for thirty-five years, tells me one day in his office.

"I was asked to speak at a meeting of key leaders in San Diego," he says. "I decided to accept even though it upended my schedule. It meant a chartered plane, an overnight flight, and little time except to shower and shave."

Father went and spoke out about the escalating nuclear arms race.

Hesburgh continues: "One week later, my secretary tells me Joan Kroc is on the phone. I don't know any Joan Kroc, I tell her. She says, 'Father, I think you should take this call.'

"I pick up the phone and Mrs. Kroc tells me she wants to see me. She comes. She's sitting right where you're sitting, Jerry.

"'Father,' she says to me, 'it was only by chance I was in San Diego at the meeting where you spoke. I was so taken by what you said that I'd like to give $6 million to Notre Dame.' And she did."

(Mrs. Kroc, of the McDonalds fortune, made an additional $6 million gift two years later to build the Hesburgh Center for International Studies. On the occasion of Father Hesburgh's eighty-sixth birthday, she gave $5 million for scholarships. And in 2003, a $50 million bequest from Mrs. Kroc—the single largest gift in the history of Notre Dame—was directed to the Kroc Institute on Notre Dame's campus.)

"And that's the sort of thing that's always happening to me," Father told me at the time. "It's just plain luck."

But luck doesn't seem to be accidental. The great fundraisers have the knack of being at the right place at the right time. That's clearly what Louis Pasteur meant when he said, "Luck favors the prepared mind."

Chapter 25

The Perils of Mediocrity

Dick DeVos is the son of the co-founder of Amway. Not an easy mantle being in the shadow of Richard DeVos, one of the nation's premier marketing geniuses.

Dick worked every possible job at Amway before becoming head of the International Division. Under his leadership, international revenue grew from 5 percent of Amway's revenue to 50 percent. His focus was always on excellence—for him personally and for all in the division.

This personal drive carries over to the many organizations he's involved with. For example, he chaired the Foundation of Spectrum Health in Grand Rapids, Michigan, one of the nation's largest health systems.

"I wanted every board member to know that in our decisions and in our solicitations, we sought excellence," he tells me. "An interesting thing happens when excellence becomes your core value. It permeates everything you do, even the way you solicit."

The campaign goal was $110 million for Spectrum's Children's Hospital. Dick's persistence and commitment were unrelenting. A total of $140 million was raised.

John Edmund Haggai is the amazing founder of the Haggai Institute, a global organization that trains leaders to transform the world they live in for Christ. In its fifty years, the institute has raised over a billion dollars. John has raised most of that himself.

"I'm on fire for what we do," he tells me. "I love asking for money for our cause because I know it's for the Lord's work. For me, excellence is who I am and what I do.

"Before calling on a donor, I spend hours preparing. For any number of reasons the person may decide not to give. But it won't be because I haven't prepared."

I've discovered through the years that excellence is never an accident. It's the result of lofty objectives and aspirations that make you stand on tiptoe. And hard work that never seems to end.

Perhaps Abraham Lincoln said it best: "If I'm going to spend six hours cutting down a tree, I spend four hours of that sharpening my saw."

Chapter 26

The Devil's in the Details

"God is in the details," said Mies Van der Rohe, the award-winning architect.

Sometimes if you don't prepare, you miss a big thing. I know this from experience, I'm embarrassed to say.

Martha Ingram is on the *Forbes* list of billionaires in the country. She's one of Nashville's most generous citizens. If it's for the good of Nashville and the area, you'll find Martha in the thick of things. She's a faithful worker. A dogged and determined volunteer. And a fearless asker.

And she insists on being prepared. For Martha, nothing is left to chance.

She and I called on an elderly gentleman for the Nashville Ballet, an organization dear to Martha. The gentleman is regarded as one of the wealthiest in the state.

I thought I had prepared Martha properly. The man's net worth, giving to other organizations, his alma mater, where his kids went to school.

But it shames me to tell you I didn't examine perhaps the most important factor—his interest in the ballet. This wasn't my proudest moment.

We're sitting in this man's office chatting away. Finally, Martha says, "We're here today to talk to you about the Nashville Ballet, a great community asset and one of the most important companies in the country."

You would have had to be there to believe what comes next.

"Oh yes," the man says. "Mary and me went to the bal-let (his pronunciation) once. Martha, honey, one thing I didn't understand. They kept those poor girls on tiptoes the whole evening. If they wanted taller girls, why didn't they hire them?"

We didn't get a gift. And I received a proper scolding from Martha.

Chapter 27

Amazing What You Don't Get

Markita Andrews was thirteen years old when she was interviewed on NBC morning television. At that point, she was the all-time champion seller of Girl Scout cookies— eleven thousand boxes in a year.

Let me paraphrase the conversation.

"Markita," Bryant Gumbel asks, "how did you sell all those Girl Scout Cookies?"

"Well," she says, "you can't just stand around. There comes a time when you have to stop chatting. You've got to look them in the eye and ask them to buy your cookies."

That's it. A young teenager knows the secret. You've got to ask for the order. Always keep that in mind.

Walter Lippman was one of America's most notable writers, reporters, and commentators of the 20th century. His biographer, Ronald Steel, once asked Lippman why he gave all of his papers and memorabilia to Yale. He was, after all, a graduate of Harvard and a member of the Harvard Board of Overseers.

According to Steel, Harvard assumed it would get Lippman's papers. But it never formally approached him. Never asked.

The moral of the story? Yale did ask and got the papers. It even got his beloved baseball hat!

Many organizations don't lack a culture of philanthropy. They lack a culture of asking.

In study after study, when people are asked why they haven't made a gift to an organization, the response voiced most often is that they weren't asked.

I called on Frank for a major university. Through our research we discovered his net worth was north of $100 million. But he had never given a dime to his alma mater. My first question when I'm sitting in his office is, "How did you happen to go to the university?" It turns out he grew up on a farm. No money at all.

"But I'll tell you how lucky I was. I got a full scholarship for four years including room and board."

(This is going quite well so far!)

"How was the experience?" I ask.

"It was the greatest thing in my life," gushes Frank. "It turned me inside out. Look where I am today. I owe it to the university. And the added bonus—I met my wife there."

(It couldn't have been going any better. I'm doing mental high-fives.)

We continue talking about how much the university means to him. He mentions a favorite faculty member, a retired professor with whom he still corresponds.

We spent more than an hour chatting about his family, his interests, the local organizations he's involved with. I learn he's a venture capitalist. It's not a world I'm very familiar with, so I probe.

"How many deals do you do in a typical year?" Frank tells me usually about five.

I lean forward and ask in a quiet way, "How much do you usually make on a deal?" (Yes, I did really ask the question.) Frank tells me it's usually around $5 million.

"For all the university means to you—your wife and family, your success, everything you are—would you give one of these deals to the university?"

That wasn't even a proper ask. I wait. I wait. "Yes, Jerry, I'll do that," Frank says.

Later, when I ask why he's never given to the university before, here's what he says: "You know, it's interesting. No one has ever asked me."

Always keep Frank in mind. You'll be hurt more by those who would have said yes, but weren't asked, than by those who told you no.

Chapter 28

Listen the Gift

You probably know the definition of an anagram. It means two words that have different meanings but contain the same letters. The words *listen* and *silent* are a good example. And how entirely appropriate that these two are an anagram.

When visiting a would-be donor, every communication skill is valued. Verbal competency is what helps propel prospective donors to action. A dazzling presentation can help. But the most important communication skill is what Quakers call devout listening.

You listen with your eyes, with your entire body. It requires a tremendous amount of energy.

Vartan Gregorian, whom I mentioned earlier, told me this: "The ability to communicate is essential to being a great fundraiser. I can be persuasive. I can even inspire. But most of all, the reason I feel I'm successful is that I'm a good listener."

You've heard about people who talk too much. But you've never heard of anyone listening too much. In fundraising, it is impossible to listen too much.

The problem is that too many people listen to respond. The successful fundraiser listens to gain information.

If you do most of the talking, you're in the spotlight—it's *your* agenda. You're not picking up clues. You're not learning anything new. You're dominating the conversation instead of guiding it.

Some CEOs are poor listeners. I can partly understand that. The university president, the hospital administrator, the Salvation Army colonel—they're always at center stage. They need a commanding presence. It's showtime.

But that can be a hindrance.

The president of a Midwestern university and I are calling on a wealthy alumnus (he's listed in *Forbes*). We believe he feels positive about the university, but no one has called on him to test that assumption. And since he was a star football player during his university days, we think he'll be interested in giving to the sports center. But no one has tested that either.

As you would expect, I coached the president. We want to get Phil to talk, I told him. We need to bring him out. Probe for what interests him. But the president didn't listen. On our visit, he rambled on and on about the university and what he wanted to do.

Afterwards, in the car, he said, "That was a really good session, wasn't it?" I'm the consultant. I need to be honest.

"You didn't probe. You didn't find out if Phil has any concerns or issues with the university. We didn't discover what's going on in his world. We didn't learn how interested he might be in the sports center."

I could have said more, but I didn't. Need I tell you we didn't get the gift?

Remember what Montaigne said, that what a person wants most in life is to be heard.

Chapter 29

It's Everything

Integrity is the *sine qua non* in our work. The indispensable fabric of all we do. All we are.

I ask highly successful fundraisers what they consider the distinguishing feature in their work. Virtually all said integrity.

I ask major donors, "What is the most important quality you look for in a fundraiser?" They too tell me—integrity. They must have abiding and unshakable faith in the person making the call. If you can't believe the messenger, you can't believe the message.

"Reputation," Thomas Paine wrote, "is what others think of you. Integrity and your true character is what God and the angels know of you." Often in one's life, you stand on the isthmus. There is destiny's choice of going one way or the other.

It can be a scorching test of character, but if you have integrity, you do what is right, even —and especially—when no one is looking.

Let me tell you about an evening I'll never forget.

I'm having dinner with the late Bill Bright. It's at a Marriott in Irvine, California. Bill was founder of Campus Crusade (now known as Cru) and author of many books. He was regarded as one of the most important ambassadors of the Christian faith in the last half of the twentieth century. Bill and his wife, Vonette, spent more than half a century building Cru to its current size of more than 27,000 staff members and 225,000 volunteers working in 190 countries.

As dinner is being served, I'm wondering what is the one question most likely to touch Bill's heart. What can I ask this most highly esteemed Christian? Then it dawns on me.

"Bill, tell me when you first met Jesus Christ?" We spent three hours at the table talking about his journey. Part of the time tears streamed down his cheeks.

"I grew up as a pagan," he tells me. "Now I'm a slave to Christ. I have only one uncompromising passion. That is to take the Gospel of Christ to the world."

We get to talking about giving and philanthropy. After all, that's why I was there. Allow me to paraphrase our conversation.

"You're raising over $300 million a year in gifts," I say to Bill. "How much of that do you get involved in?"

"I have a wonderful staff. But I'm directly involved with probably the top fifty donors. They like to see me."

"Do you have any trouble in asking?"

"It's funny," Bill says. "Actually, I don't have to ask. I tell them about our work and our outreach. And the checks come streaming in." If that sounds familiar, it's exactly what Vartan Gregorian told me about his work at the New York Public Library—that he didn't have to ask.

It's quiet for a moment. Bill gives some thought to what he's going to say next.

"Actually, I think it's all about trust and integrity," he tells me. "My values. I believe donors have confidence in me as the Lord's envoy."

The poet Martin Tupper wrote that integrity is "a call that ignites the spirit." You are in charge of your life. You are one with Gandhi, who said: "My life is its own message."

Afterword

When we started this journey, I promised I would describe the qualities that make a singularly successful fundraiser. I've kept faith with you.

It was like origami when I began. I folded a piece here, slid a piece there. Angled this piece and tilted this one. But bit by bit it all came together.

And have you noticed something? Few of these qualities we've discussed are inherent. They can be learned. Of course it won't be easy. A brook would lose its song if God removed the rocks.

Charles Payne is a television host. He knows hard times, having lived in poverty and faced his share of struggles. His godson, just out of college, visited one day and bemoaned to Payne that he couldn't land a job. He applied often but was never accepted.

Let me paraphrase their conversation.

"I don't understand," Payne said. "Your grades are excellent, good school, and you have a certain presence.

There's only one thing I can think of. What do you wear to the interviews?"

"What I have on now," said his godson, which was a black shirt and tie.

"A black shirt?" said an incredulous Payne. "Don't you know any better?"

"I only have a black shirt," replied the young man. "I can't afford another shirt."

That's when Payne decided to start Shirt and Tie for Success, an organization offering a white shirt and a tie to those who need them for an interview. With the help of his wife and sister-in law, Paine bought fifty shirts and ties and visited several schools in the Bronx. He spoke with principals and guidance counselors, who then connected him to students who gave him their résumés and received their shirts and ties. Even providing a white shirt and tie provides a never-ending ripple in philanthropy.

But first you must begin. And with fierce urgency. The greatest sin is to have a good impulse and fail to act on it.

You and I together have made beautiful music. I think of the popular World War I song, "Till We Meet Again. . . ."

About the Author

A fundraiser for more than four decades, Jerold Panas is the executive director of Jerold Panas, Linzy & Partners, which has more than 60 staff and has served over 3,500 organizations since its founding in 1968. During his career, he personally has helped raise an estimated $11 billion for a wide variety of charitable organizations, including many around the world.

Panas is widely regarded as the foremost author on fundraising, having written or co-written 19 books on the subject, as well as countless articles for magazines, newsletters, and newspapers around the world. His book, *Asking*, is the bestselling fundraising book of all time. Others such as *Mega Gifts*, *The Fundraising Habits of Supremely Successful Boards*, and *Making a Case Your Donors Will Love* are classics and standards for the profession.

Recently, Panas was recipient of the prestigious Chair's Award for Outstanding Service presented by the Association of Fundraising Professionals (AFP).

Other Jerold Panas Books Published by Emerson & Church

Asking

A 59-Minute Guide to Everything Board Members, Volunteers, and Staff Must Know to Secure the Gift

Mega Gifts

Who Gives Them, Who Gets Them

The Fundraising Habits of Supremely Successful Boards

A 59-Minute Guide to Assuring Your Organization's Future

Making a Case Your Donors Will Love

The Secret to Selling the Dream

The Gold Standard in Board Books

Asking Jerold Panas, 112 pp., $24.95, ISBN 9781889102498

It ranks right up there with public speaking. Nearly all of us fear it. And yet it's critical to our success. *Asking for money*. This landmark book convincingly shows that nearly everyone, regardless of their persuasive ability, can become an effective fundraiser if they follow Jerold Panas' step-by-step guidelines.

The Ultimate Board Member's Book
Kay Sprinkel Grace, 120 pp., $24.95, ISBN 9781889102481

A book for *all* nonprofit boards: those wanting to operate with maximum effectiveness, those needing to clarify exactly what their job is, and, those wanting to ensure that all members are 'on the same page.' It's all here in jargon-free language: how boards work, what the job entails, the time commitment, the role of staff, effective recruiting, de-enlisting board members, and more.

How to Raise $1 Million (or More) in 10 Bite-Sized Steps
Andrea Kihlstedt 104 pp., $24.95, ISBN 9781889102412

Raising a million dollars is easier than you think, says Andrea Kihlstedt. It's a matter of simplifying the process. Do that and you expel the anxiety. Kihlstedt prescribes 10 bite-sized steps. And with nearly three decades of experience and scores of campaigns to draw from, she has plenty of street cred.

The Board Member's Easier Than You Think Guide to Nonprofit Finances
Andy Robinson & Nancy Wasserman, 111 pp., $24.95, ISBN 9781889102436

With the possible exception of "How do I avoid fundraising?" a board member's most commonly unasked question is, "What do all these numbers mean, and what am I supposed to do with them?" Financial planning and budgeting combine all of our money taboos with that common math disorder, math phobia. But authors Andy Robinson and Nancy Wasserman help trustees and their staff colleagues confront and address this fear - with wisdom, clarity, humor, and humility.

The Gold Standard in Board Books

The 11 Questions Every Donor Asks
Harvey McKinnon, 112 pp., $24.95, ISBN 9781889102542

A watershed book, *The 11 Questions* prepares you for the tough questions you'll inevitably face from prospective donors. Harvey McKinnon identifies 11 such questions, ranging from "Why me?" to "Will my gift make a difference?" to "Will I have a say over how you use my gift?"

The Fundraising Habits of Supremely Successful Boards
Jerold Panas, 108 pp., $24.95, ISBN 9781889102474

In his storied career, Jerold Panas has worked with more than 3,000 boards, all the while helping them to surpass their campaign goals of $100,000 to $100 million. Funnel every ounce of that experience and wisdom into a single book and what you end up with is *The Fundraising Habits of Supremely Successful Boards*, the brilliant culmination of what Panas has learned firsthand about boards that excel at the task of resource development.

How to Make Your Board Dramatically More Effective, Starting Today Gayle Gifford, 114 pp., $24.95, ISBN 9781889102450

This could be the most productive hour your board ever spends. Sixty minutes is all it takes to read *How to Make Your Board Dramatically More Effective, Starting Today*.Gayle Gifford poses a host of key questions. By answering them, your board can tell instantly what it's doing right, what's it's doing wrong, and where it can stand improvement.Suited to any board that isn't perfect.

Fundraising Mistakes that Bedevil All Boards (and Staff Too)
Kay Sprinkel Grace 110 pp., $24.95, ISBN 9781889102405

Over the past 70 years, organizations of all kinds have tested literally hundreds of fundraising techniques and strategies. Some have succeeded beyond expectations, but too many approaches have failed The result? Untold hours are wasted, causes go unfunded, and disappointment and frustration demoralize volunteers and staff everywere. Grace seeks to end these costly blunders once and for all.

www.emersonandchurch.com

Copies of this and other books from the publisher are available at discount when purchased in quantity for boards of directors or staff. Call 508-359-0019 or visit www.emersonandchurch.com.

15 Brook Street – Medfield, MA 02052
Tel. 508-359-0019
www.emersonandchurch.com